Jacob's Well Publishing
45 Buford Lane
Poplarville, Mississippi 39470
wwwjacobswellrecoverycenter.com

Scriptures referred to in this book are taken from the most up to date translation of the New International Version of the Holy Bible published by Zondervan Publishing House and provided on line by biblegateway.com

First published by Jacobs Well Publishing
February 2016

ISBN-13: 978-0692629222
ISBN-10: 069262922X

Printed in the United States of America

Editing Consultant – Julie Keene
Cover Art contributed by Artist: Ben Lichius

WHAT I LEARNED IN THE VALLEY

{The Keys to Victorious Living}

Pastor Charlie Haynes

Dedication

This book is first of all dedicated to my unbelievable and incredible family – specifically my wife Pam and my four children Virginia, Tammy, Susan and Asa – whose loving, forgiving and merciful hearts allowed me to retake a position as loving husband and father that I had foolishly thrown away and in no way deserved to be given back.

This book is further dedicated to the thousands of men and women and the families they represent that have been willing FIRST to share their hopelessness, their desperation, their fear and their failures with me but SECOND and most importantly to share their VICTORIES with me as they walked away from a life of drug addiction to take their rightful place in a new life in Christ.

This book is dedicated to those that have prayed prayers of protection over our ministry over the last fifteen years – knowing that we are rising to our feet every morning to fight the "good fight" against those things of Hell that are focused on destroying our families, our cities, our states and our nation.

But most of all this book is dedicated to my Lord and Savior Christ Jesus who loved me enough to suffer and die on the Cross of Calvary so that in spite of my sick and depraved behaviors in life, I could be forgiven. Without His direct intervention in my life NONE of the other dedications on this page would have been possible.

A little about the author: Pastor Charlie Haynes

I was born in Stamford, Texas in 1944 and shortly thereafter moved to Meridian, Mississippi where I grew up. I attended Highland Elementary, Kate Griffin Junior High, and Meridian High School and went on to four years at Livingston State Teachers College in Livingston, Alabama {now called UWA}. After leaving college I entered the field of retail management with F.W. Woolworth, then Woolco, then TG & Y, Wal-Mart, and finally Marvin's Home Center Stores. That career spanned over 30 years of my life. Early in my career {1966} I married my wife Pamela Smith Haynes from Shucktown, Ms. {that's right she was a country girl}. We have four children – Virginia, Tammy, Susan and Asa.

Unfortunately, for me and particularly for my wife and family, I began a downward spiral over those 30 years that led me into behaviors centered totally on the lust of my eyes, the needs of my flesh and the pride of life that turned me into a dark and depraved man, husband and father. In June of 1996 two weeks before Father's Day, when my family could take it no longer, my wife asked for a divorce – my children basically disowned me and then ordered me to get out and don't come back. Only then did I become willing to accept how deep into depravity I had sunk.

And just when I thought all was lost, I met a man named Jesus Christ. He has not only saved me, saved my marriage and my family but He has literally transformed me into a totally new creation. What I once thought was the end of everything, I now know was THE BEGINNING of everything.

Because I am so grateful for His mercy and loving kindness, I have purposed along with my wife and family to spend the rest of my days on this earth sharing the Good News with hopeless and hurting individuals and families, that no matter how bad it seems – Christ can redeem it, heal it and restore it. Hence my wife Pam and I founded Righteous Oaks Recovery Center for Men in Chunky, Ms in 2001, Jacob's Well Recovery Center for Women in Poplarville, Ms in 2005 and Praise God this year we have founded our second Men's Recovery Center also here in Poplarville called Damascus Road Recovery Center for Men.

Fun Things I Do: When I'm looking for something to pass the few "leisure hours" I have these days it's going to generally be spending some quality time with my precious wife Pam or brain storming with my youngest daughter and son who now serve in our ministry with us. And there's nothing like relaxing on the front porch of our little log cabin house on the lake with a cup of hot coffee and watching the fish jump.

Favorite Books: Obviously my favorite Book is the Holy Bible. But, I love surrounding myself with any and all other books that will lead me to a better understanding and Daily Application of God's Word. I'm going to be surrounded by Bible Dictionaries, Concordances, Commentaries and the writings of great men and women of God who know how to share, not only the Theology of the Word, but the daily application of it as well.

My Heart's Desire: I live my life today with the assurance of my Salvation, the living proof of my transformation and a burning desire to rise from my bed EVERY morning with only one prayer in my heart: "Lord until you bring me home to be with you for eternity, do not let one day go by that you do not place a broken hurting person in my path that I can give the same hope that you have given me in Christ Jesus, Amen."

WHAT I LEARNED IN THE VALLEY

{The Keys to Victorious Living}

PART ONE
THE INTRODUCTION

In the Spring of 1996, at 52 years of age, I experienced the "Rock Bottom" moment of my life. My wife of 30 years and three of my four children set me down at our dining room table two weeks before Fathers Day and confronted me with the ever increasing depths that I had sunk to in my behaviors as a man, a husband, a father and friend. I had fallen into the depths of alcoholism, drug use, pornography, sexual perversion and dishonest living. The result of that meeting was that my wife rose from the table and demanded an immediate end to our 30 year marriage. My three children rose from that same table and declared that they had disowned me as a father - promised I would never hold my grandchildren - and demanded that I pack up immediately and leave the premises - the further the better. As I threw my belongings in the back of my old 1988 Isuzu pick up and headed off to "nowhere" I thought it was the end of everything. BUT NOW – I know that it was actually the BEGINNING OF EVERYTHING. Two months later, I met a man who made me a solemn promise, that if I would just place my life in His hands, He would repair and restore and resurrect everything I had so foolishly thrown away. That man's name is Jesus Christ. And I know now that when He said in His Word in Jeremiah 29 that "He had a plan to prosper me – not to harm me and to give me a hope and a future"- He intended to keep the promise. That life changing night that I found myself on my knees crying out to God for forgiveness for what I had made of my life and received Christ into my heart as my Lord and Savior, I MEANT what I was saying and I MEANT what I was promising. In that moment, the pride and arrogance and ignorance that had driven me to the depths of depravity were GONE and all that was left on the floor was a broken man with a willing heart – and THAT my friends was all Christ had been waiting for.

Now almost twenty years later as I look forward to celebrating my fiftieth wedding anniversary with the precious wife Christ placed back in my life and find my relationship with the children who disowned me restored by His decree and look at the pictures of the times I got to hold my twelve grandchildren and three great grandchildren – I smile and say: "God, I didn't understand it then but I understand now why you said in:

1Corinthians 2:9 – *"As it is written: No eye has seen, no ear has heard, no mind has conceived what God has prepared for those who love Him, but God has revealed it to us by His Spirit."*

This book is inspired by some of the most important life lesson God has shown me over the years "by His Spirit." He has shown me that Membership in a Church can't "save me". My Preacher can't "save me". My perfect Sunday School Attendance Pin, my Baptism Certificate, my Political Position in Church Leadership or my Cornbread Recipe in my Congregations latest Cook Book can't "save me". Only an intimate, personal, one on one relationship with God through Christ Jesus can "save you". And that relationship will only exist if you spend a great deal of your time dedicated to being in His Word EVERY DAY for the rest of your life – READING IT – STUDYING IT – APPLYING IT and fervently praying to God to give you REVELATION KNOWLEDGE from His Word that will apply uniquely to His purpose and plan for YOUR life {your Destiny}.

This book is the result of what God has revealed to me personally through revelations He has given me in His Word concerning "The Keys to Living a Victorious Life". If like me you have lived much of your life defeated by the circumstances you have found yourself in, then I pray what I am sharing with you here will help you understand the power of what we can learn in the "valleys" of life.

PART TWO
THE JOURNEY BEGINS

One of the most powerful and life changing things God has revealed to me through His Word came from a very familiar – often quoted Scripture – The 23rd Psalm. But it was verse four of those Scriptures which declares:

*"Yea, though I walk through the Valley of the Shadow of Death, **I will fear no evil**"*

It is where God began to help me understand a very important journey I was going to have to undertake if I was going to allow Him to carry me from the desperation and despair I had placed myself in to a place of victorious daily living as a man, a father, a husband and friend. And this was the revelation He gave me: Charlie Haynes, you will never be able to walk through the "Valley of the Shadow of Death" – **WITHOUT FEAR** until you have FIRST walked through "The Valley of Dry Bones" – "Spiritual Warfare Training" and fought in "The Valley of Elah" - with **ME!**

Why "The Valley of Dry Bones"? Because the first thing we MUST do to begin the journey from Despair to Victory is to come face to face with the truth about what we have allowed ourselves to become – and the damage we have caused those who depended on and loved us as well. The truth HURTS….but God promises us in John 8:31-32:

*"If you hold to my teaching, you are really my disciples. Then you will know the truth and **the truth will set you free**."*

Trust me when I tell you that I have never had to face anything more painful than letting God take me on a tour of "The Valley of Bones" as it related to <u>MY</u> life. Have you got the courage to take that walk with Him? I wonder...

PART THREE
THE VALLEY OF DRY BONES
{Ezekiel 37:1-14-NIV}

1 The hand of the Lord was on me,

What an incredibly painful and heartbreaking moment it is when we find ourselves down on our knees in the middle of the floor with tears pouring down our cheeks – snot dripping from our nose and the sound of imperceptible moans rising from the depths of our soul because of the guilt we feel concerning where life has brought us.

That helpless moment when you suddenly come to your senses and realize and begin to take responsibility for the fact that you have carelessly thrown away everything God has given you – your life, your hopes, your plans, your family, your friends, your character and your reputation – GONE! And then in that moment – a moment where you honestly don't care whether or not you keep on breathing and mutter the words under your breath – "I can't live like this anymore," you suddenly hear the voice of God softly whisper – "Have you had enough?" And as you wipe the tears from your eyes and answer quickly – "YES LORD!" you feel His hand placed gently on your shoulder to comfort you and you hear Him say: "I have been waiting patiently all this time to hear you say those two important words – "YES LORD!" Now, rise to your feet my child – wipe away your tears, lift your head high and pull your shoulders back; follow **ME** and I will show you the pathway toward and give you the keys to victorious living.

I lived through these terrible moments twenty years ago. And as I rose to my feet, as God instructed me to, I'm sure

I had my doubts that it could ever be any different BUT I can tell you now by experiencing Him – when you say YES to God – everything He promises – <u>HE DELIVERS</u>!!!

and he brought me out by the Spirit of the Lord and set me in the middle of a valley; it was full of bones.

It's those first steps on the journey that God must take you on that are by far the most painful you will ever take – because you are starting that journey on the "Road to Redemption."

The definition of the word <u>REDEMPTION</u> is: to make amends or reparation, for a fault, mistake, offense or crime that you have committed.

Just taking the first step in this part of the journey will be impossible if you are not willing to understand that you are getting ready to be asked my God Almighty to walk out every inch of this road by walking only in the <u>TRUTH</u> while taking <u>TOTAL</u> and <u>COMPLETE</u> <u>RESPONSIBILITY</u> for where you have found yourself in life AND the pain and heartbreak you have caused those who love you. No more excuses. No more blaming everyone else for you problems in life. It's all just about <u>YOU</u> looking deep into your own soul and saying: "I know it was me Lord. Please forgive me and give me another chance to get this right." He will say: "<u>No problem</u>".

[2] He led me back and forth among them, and I saw a great many bones on the floor of the valley, bones that were very dry.

The "Road to Redemption" runs directly through the "Valley of Dry Bones" and as God led me through He said: "My son what do you see before you?" And I looked and I said: "Just looks like a bunch of bones to me and there very dry and brittle." God lovingly slipped His arm around my shoulder – smiled – and said: "You need to take responsibility for the bones and look again." So I did as He instructed – I took responsibility and looked again and suddenly shame and remorse overtook me as I realized that here on the floor of the valley were the dead, dry and crumbled remains of what was once my thirty year marriage I had thrown away. There in another pile were the dead and dying remains of the relationship I could have had with my children and grandchildren. There were dry bones all about me –from the death of my friendships, my future, my hopes, my character and my reputation and more. It was an overwhelming sight. It was a field of destruction so vast and so devastating I could see no way out.

And then, all of a sudden, God asked me a LIFE CHANGING question…

³ He asked me, "Son of man, can these bones live?"

And of course my immediate gut reaction was probably the same as yours would be – "<u>Lord, are you serious</u>???" But respectfully I answered:

"Sovereign Lord, you alone know."

Suddenly God shocked me by revealing to me that not only could I be instrumental in repairing and restoring His plan for my life but further that He **expected me to** when He said to me:

*⁴ "**<u>You prophesy</u>** to these bones and say to them, 'Dry bones; hear the word of the Lord!*

Praise God and Hallelujah! God suddenly reminded me that His Word is –" living and active." Sharper than any double edged sword, penetrating even to the dividing of soul and spirit, joints and marrow; it judges the thoughts and attitudes of the heart." {Hebrews 4:12}

He further reminded me that He has given me divine authority through His power – the Blood of Christ – the presence of the Holy Spirit and the Truth of His Word to rebuke and expel the things of Hell and call down the things of Heaven on my own life. In Matthew 18:18 Jesus said:

"I tell you the truth, whatever __you__ bind on earth will be bound in Heaven, and whatever __you__ loose on earth will be loosed in Heaven.

God was giving me a powerful piece of information about life I did not know. And that was - instead of spending the rest of my life wallowing in my misery – blaming everyone else for my problems and calling down curses on myself and my family by agreeing with Satan that all was lost, I needed to start calling down blessing and healing and forgiveness and reconciliation and joy and peace and love and honor and redemption on my life, my marriage, my family and my future.

*[5] This is what the Sovereign Lord told me to say to these bones {**broken circumstances**}:*

*"I will make breath enter you {**give you a new hope**},*

*and you will come to life {**another chance**}.*

*[6] I will attach tendons to you {**reunite where reunification is needed**}*

and make flesh come upon you {**restore where restoration is needed**}

and cover you with skin {**repair where reparation is needed**};

I will put breath in you {**fill you with the power and presence of the Holy Spirit**},

and you will come to life. {**You will rise from the ashes of sin and death to take your rightful place in the Kingdom of God**}

Then you will know that I am the Lord.'"

[7] *So I prophesied as I was commanded. And as I was prophesying, there was a noise, a rattling sound, and the bones* ***started coming together****, bone to bone.*

I underlined the phrase "started coming together" for a very specific reason. I had to learn by experience that when God starts a healing work in your life and your family, it is not done instantaneously. It will be done in HIS time and in HIS way so we must be patient. We are living in an "I want it right now world" but we are serving a "when I'M ready God." But I can tell you that he immediately began the process of reconciliation of my marriage, family life and future the moment I surrendered in obedience to HIS will and HIS plan. He began to reconnect broken and dry bones of my past one at a time in the order of His choice.

[8] *I looked, and tendons and flesh appeared on them and skin covered them, BUT*

*- **there was no breath in them.***

Oh, wait a minute God! You said there was going to be breath in them God. Everything was moving along fine so where's the breath you promised? When God isn't moving things as quickly as we think he should, and worse than that, we too quickly begin to forget His previous instructions – don't worry – he will remind us.

Hey son, have you so quickly forgotten my advice and counsel. I told you I was expecting **YOU** to take responsibility for your problems and for **YOU** to declare a blessing over the healing of your circumstances. What are you looking at me for? Get to blessing son!

> [9] Then he said to me, *"**YOU** prophesy to the breath; prophesy, son of man, and say to it, 'This is what the Sovereign Lord says: Come, breath, from the four winds and breathe into these slain, that they may live.'"* [10] *So I prophesied as he commanded me, and breath entered them;*

Just as He promised it would…

Even today all these years later, when I complain because I don't think God is moving fast enough in my circumstances, He smiles and gently speaks this question: "Hey son, you better double check and see who's waiting on who." And then there is this last powerful life changing part of Verse 10 that I never saw coming when I first trod the "Valley of Dry Bones" with God -

> *"And the bones came to life and stood up on their feet—**a vast army**."*

There is an army rising up!!!

{More about the "vast army" later in the book}

The "Valley of Dry Bones" experience will be one of the hardest things you will ever undertake in your life. BUT, when you come out on the other side, you will be **FREE** once and for all from the guilt and shame of your former life because you will know that you know that you have taken full responsibility for the sins of your past – confessed them before your Father in Heaven –repented of them in an honest moment of what the Word calls "Godly Sorrow" and received His forgiveness through the Blood Sacrifice of His Son Christ Jesus.

2 Corinthians 7:10 (NIV) [10] Godly sorrow brings repentance that leads to salvation and leaves no regret, but worldly sorrow brings death.

More importantly there is a freedom that comes with taking all the mistakes and misbehaviors and misjudgements of your life and placing them at the Foot of the Cross and leaving them there. Now you can consider them "water under the bridge" as far as God is concerned and understand further that it is only what concerns God {not man}that matters anyway. Now you can cling to this Word of encouragement God whispered into my spirit twenty years ago: "Charlie Haynes, it is not what you have DONE in life that defines you. Rather, it is what you have done ABOUT what you have done that defines you. My son, never let the shame of your past stand in the way of your future in Christ."

God's Word best summarizes the results of walking through the "Valley of Bones" this way in Psalms 32:1-11

¹ Blessed is the one
whose transgressions are forgiven,
whose sins are covered.
² Blessed is the one
whose sin the Lord does not count against them
and in whose spirit is no deceit.

³ When I kept silent,
my bones wasted away
through my groaning all day long.
⁴ For day and night
your hand was heavy on me;
my strength was sapped
as in the heat of summer.

⁵ Then I acknowledged my sin to you
and did not cover up my iniquity.
I said, "I will confess
my transgressions to the Lord."
And you forgave
the guilt of my sin.

⁶ Therefore let all the faithful pray to you
while you may be found;
surely the rising of the mighty waters
will not reach them.
⁷ You are my hiding place;
you will protect me from trouble
and surround me with songs of deliverance.

⁸ I will instruct you and teach you in the way you should
go;
I will counsel you with my loving eye on you.
⁹ Do not be like the horse or the mule,

which have no understanding
but must be controlled by bit and bridle
or they will not come to you.

[10] Many are the woes of the wicked, but the Lord's
unfailing love surrounds the one who trusts in him.
[11] Rejoice in the Lord and be glad, you righteous; sing, all
you who are upright in heart!

So, the question of the day is: What hopeless, helpless, destructive and seemingly undefeatable thing or things are present in your life right now that God Almighty is prompting you to prophesy against and what are you going to do about it? Your life changing journey awaits – There is the Road to Redemption and the first valley just beyond. One step at a time my friend – one step at a time.

Now that you are free from your past, you must now be willing to allow God to prepare you for the battle that lies ahead.

Time for "Spiritual Warfare Training"

No self respecting soldier in the Army of God would step onto the battlefield without the proper mental, physical, emotional and spiritual battle gear. It is vitally important that God briefs us in advance what kind of battle we are entering. Here's what He tells us about "The Battle" in 2 Corinthians 10:3-5 (NIV)

[3] For though we live in the world, we do not wage war as the world does. [4] The weapons we fight with are not the weapons of the world. On the contrary, they have divine power to demolish strongholds. [5] We demolish arguments and every pretension that sets itself up against the knowledge of God, and we take captive every thought to make it obedient to Christ.

PART FOUR
ARMOR UP!!
Ephesians 6:10-18

{The Armor of God}

*[10] **Finally**, be strong in **the Lord** and in **His mighty power**.*

Imagine with me for just a moment. You have just successfully completed one of the longest and hardest journeys you have ever taken in life – that painful walk with God Almighty along the "Road to Redemption" and straight through the "Valley of Bones." You have had to face every failure, every bad choice, and every moment of depravity, every wrong turn and every disastrous consequence of your old life and **FINALLY** take responsibility for it and put it behind you forever. You have received in your heart and stand on the truth of God's Word that says:

[62] "No one who puts a hand to the plow and looks back is fit for service in the Kingdom of God."{Luke 9:62 (NIV)}

And, you have absolutely no intention of looking back over your shoulder at your past or allowing it to control your future. Because you know without doubt that those things no longer control **YOU**. They no longer define you. They no longer strike fear in your heart or give you fear of what the future holds for you and your family.

Now, weary from the journey you suddenly find yourself sitting at the feet of God. He leans forward on His throne – smiles and says one of the most important –most life changing single words you will ever hear – **FINALLY!!!**

Webster's definition of the word "finally" indicates that it means: eventually, after considerable delay or at last. The Greek word used in the original scripture for the word "finally" is "loipon" which in the Greek is translated as "it remains then."

Everything else you have tried has failed – CHRIST REMAINS!!!

{NOTE: God waited patiently for 52 years for me to come to my "FINALLY" moment. How long has He been patiently waiting for you?}

Finally, you have hit "Rock Bottom." Finally, you are ready to listen to the Truth of God instead of the lies of the world. Finally, you are ready to admit and take personal responsibility for your past behavior. Finally, you are willing to accept the truth that God created you for a purpose and a destiny and YOU AIN'T IN IT!

28 And we know that in all things God works for the good of those who love him, who have been called according to His purpose. {Romans 8:28 (NIV)}

And most pleasing to God, you have FINALLY decided in truth and in faith to:

"Be strong in <u>the Lord</u> and in <u>His mighty power</u>."

Because you are now in a position to accept the advice in Jeremiah 17 that he has been trying to place in your heart forever which says:

⁵ This is what the Lord says:

"Cursed is the one who trusts in man,
who draws strength from mere flesh
and whose heart turns away from the Lord.
⁶ That person will be like a bush in the wastelands;
they will not see prosperity when it comes.
They will dwell in the parched places of the desert,
in a salt land where no one lives.
⁷ "But blessed is the one who trusts in the Lord,
whose confidence is in him.
⁸ They will be like a tree planted by the water
that sends out its roots by the stream.
It does not fear when heat comes;
its leaves are always green.
It has no worries in a year of drought
and never fails to bear fruit."

One of the most difficult truths that I had to learn to accept about life is: That I am not now nor have I ever been in charge of my life, my future or my destiny. I am caught in the middle of a raging battle in the heavenlies for my very soul. At some point I was going to have to make a life changing decision to <u>surrender</u>. The question is: WHO am I going to chose to surrender too? God's Word tells me in the Book of John that I only have two choices.

42 Jesus said to them, "If <u>God</u> were your Father, you would love me, for I have come here from God. I have not come on my own; God sent me. 43 Why is my language not clear to you? Because you are unable to hear what I say. 44 You belong to your father, <u>the devil</u>, and you want to carry out your father's desires. He was a murderer from the beginning, not holding to the truth, for there is no truth in him. When he lies, he speaks his native language, for he is a liar and the father of lies. 45 Yet because I tell the truth, you do not believe me! {John 8:42-45}

Unfortunately, for most of my adult life I chose to allow Satan to be my father and allowed **him** to control my life – and guess what – I became a "chip off the old block"- driven by the lust of my eyes, the needs of my flesh and the pride of life – and a "dyed in the wool" liar and manipulator. Sadly, the one person that I lied too and manipulated the most was <u>MYSELF</u>. What a wonderful day it was when I deserted the armies of Hell and joined the Army of God. I recommend it highly.

*11 **Put on the full armor** of God, so that you can take your stand against **the devil's schemes.***

The very first thing I was taught as a soldier in the Army of God was that I needed to quickly armor up for the battle and what I needed to armor up with. God placed in my spirit that Satan would never give up on chasing after me.

To him I was a deserter and therefore now a target. There would never be a day that he would stop scheming on how to take me out. But God also reminded me that because I had chosen to become the blood bought property of Jesus Christ – The devil has NO authority over me. {Except what I give him}

[7] Submit yourselves, then, to God. Resist the devil, and he will flee from you. James 4:7 (NIV)

So God, as He always has, sat me down and helped me understand not only the importance of the <u>SPIRITUAL ARMOR</u> He was offering but more importantly that the battle is **HIS** to win not mine and the **HE** will lead me to victory every time if I will put my trust and my life in **HIS** hands. Here are His words of encouragement:

[4] Almighty God will cover you with his feathers,
and under his wings you will find refuge;
his faithfulness will be your shield and rampart.
[5] You will not fear the terror of night,
nor the arrow that flies by day,
[6] nor the pestilence that stalks in the darkness,
nor the plague that destroys at midday.
[7] A thousand may fall at your side,
ten thousand at your right hand,
but it will not come near you.
[8] You will only observe with your eyes
and see the punishment of the wicked.
[9] If you say, "The Lord is my refuge,"
and you make the Most High your dwelling,
[10] no harm will overtake you,
no disaster will come near your tent.{ Psalm 91:4-10 NIV}

And here is why…

*[12] For **our struggle is not against flesh and blood**, but against the rulers, against the authorities, against the powers of this dark world and against the spiritual forces of evil in the heavenly realms.*

*[13] Therefore **put on!!!** the full armor of God,*

Why?

*so that when the day of evil comes, you may be able to stand your ground, and after you have done everything, to stand. [14] **Stand firm then!!!***

My wife and I have cable. We have over 100 different channels available to us from that provider BUT very few of them are fit to watch. Why? Because this world has become and continues to increasingly become a VERY evil place. It seems that no matter whether it's television, the internet, the radio stations, the newspapers, the magazines, the billboards or a simple stroll through the mall – we are constantly confronted with the uninvited appearance of evil. If you study God's Word you are not surprised by it because he gave us all the heads up.

We just didn't believe Him.

3 But mark this: There will be terrible times in the last days. ^{2} People will be lovers of themselves, lovers of money, boastful, proud, abusive, disobedient to their parents, ungrateful, unholy, ^{3} without love, unforgiving, slanderous, without self-control, brutal, not lovers of the good, ^{4} treacherous, rash, conceited, lovers of pleasure rather than lovers of God— ^{5} having a form of godliness but denying its power. Have nothing to do with such people.

^{6} They are the kind who worm their way into homes and gain control over gullible women, who are loaded down with sins and are swayed by all kinds of evil desires, ^{7} always learning but never able to come to a knowledge of the truth. {2 Timothy 3:1-7 (NIV)}

So, we turn on our television, pick up a newspaper, or scan the internet – and we shake our heads is in despair and disgust and complain to the person sitting alongside us: "What in the world is wrong with our country" and "What is it coming to?"

I believe that what is wrong with the United States of America, including ANY State, County, City, Township or Cross Road Community in this once great nation called America is NOT the fault of the President, NOT the fault of the Congress, NOT the fault of the Senate and NOT the fault of the Supreme Court.

The truth is that an ever increasing "moral decay" of this once great and noble nation has brought on rampant hatred and bigotry and prejudice and lying and anger and greed and selfishness and murder and rape and robbery AND the ever increasing destruction of the American family at ALL levels of our society.

And, it breaks my heart to say that this terrible dilemma that we have found ourselves in must be laid directly at the feet of those of us who openly state and profess that we are Christians BUT live our lives in desperation, defeat and hopelessness...

I'm talking about those of us who are so quick to broadcast that "Christ died for us" but in truth won't spend an hour of our time "living for Him."

I'm talking about those of us who know all the "religious" things to say around our "religious" friends but wouldn't dare to bring up Christ's name in a crowd if we thought it might offend somebody.

We have absolutely no hope of ever taking our COUNTRY back until we first decide to TAKE GOD BACK and begin to walk out the VICTORY that He has always had in store for us!!!

So, how much longer will we shake our heads in wonderment and disgust and mutter under our breath: "When is **<u>somebody</u>** going to do something about this?"

NO! The big question is – when are **<u>WE</u>** going to do something about this? When are **<u>WE</u>** going to start not only to "taking a stand" but when are we going to take that stand and "STAND FIRM" IN IT instead of moaning and complaining about the circumstances we have found ourselves in?

I've got the answer to that penetrating question. It will be when we say YES LORD! – put on the armor he has offered us and use it as He has instructed in his Word.

Weapon Number One

*with the **belt of truth** buckled around your waist,*

I have always found it interesting that the very first weapon that God says we must put on is "the belt of truth." And I have come to realize after all these years that if we are not willing to strap on that weapon first, we might as well not bother with strapping on any of the rest of it. Why? Here's Why!

[8] But for those who are self-seeking and who reject <u>the truth</u> and follow evil, there will be wrath and anger. {Romans 2:8 NIV}

[18] The wrath of God is being revealed from heaven against all the godlessness and wickedness of people, who suppress <u>the truth</u> by their wickedness, {Romans 1:18 NIV}

[23] Yet a time is coming and has now come when the true worshipers will worship the Father in the Spirit and <u>in truth</u>, for they are the kind of worshipers the Father seeks. {John 4:23 NIV}

[18] Whoever speaks on their own does so to gain personal glory, but he who seeks the glory of the one who sent him is <u>a man of truth</u>; there is nothing false about him. {John 7:18 NIV}

[13] But when he, the <u>Spirit of truth</u>, comes, he will guide you into <u>all the truth</u>. He will not speak on his own; he will

speak only what he hears, and he will tell you what is yet to come. {John 16: NIV}

⁶ Jesus answered, "I am the way and the truth and the life. No one comes to the Father except through me. {John 14:6 NIV}

Before we can effectively put on the "Belt of Truth" we must be willing to first take off the "Belt of Lies" that the devil has given us. In order to ensure that we have the ability to lie our way out of almost any situation the devil gives us at least three belts: 1.the Belt of Half-Truths {aka the "what they don't know won't hurt 'em belt"} 2.the Belt of Wicked Devices{aka the embellishment, gossip, slander and dissensions belt} 3.the Belt of Manipulation{aka the belt able to stretch and bend the truth to fit any evil circumstance}.

NOTE: WE ONLY NEED ONE BELT OF TRUTH BECAUSE NO MATTER WHO WE ARE, IT FITS JUST RIGHT!!!

Now let's talk for a minute about this thing called the "Belt of Truth"- how to put it on and how to use it.

I learned the hard way on my journey down that road from darkness to deliverance that the greatest, the most dangerous and most destructive lie we will ever tell is the one tell ourselves. In order to put on and effectively use the Belt of Truth in our life we must finally begin to take personal responsibility for who we are, what we have become, what we have done and be willing to face the consequences we have created by our own actions- <u>without blaming others.</u> You are going to have to look into what I call the spiritual mirror of life and take a long hard look at what you see in that mirror.

Don't just look into the mirror like you normally do when you fix your hair, put on your makeup, trim your beard or whatever other beautifying ritual you use the mirror for daily but rather look deep into your own soul – muster the courage to begin doing something you may have never done before – examine your heart instead of your outward appearance and behavior. A good friend once shared this little poem with me and I have held on to it and treasured it as sound wisdom:

<blockquote>
I have six honest serving men,

I'll keep them till I die.

Their names are Who and What and Where

And When and How and Why
</blockquote>

Ask yourself:

<u>**Who**</u> do you try to make others "think you are" and in reality "Who are you?"

<u>**What**</u> do you think "God created you to do" with your life and "What have you done about it?"

<u>**Where**</u> did you " hope you would find yourself at your age" and "Where are you now?"

When was the last time you told yourself – I cannot live this way anymore and "When are you really going to do something about it?"

How did you get yourself into this mess and "How are you going to get yourself out of it?"

Why have you never considered Christ Jesus as the answer and "Why don't you consider him now?"

There is an awesome life changing promise awaiting you in the "spirit mirror" of life! That promise was made in John 8:32:

"Then you will know the truth, and the truth will set you free."

Weapon Number Two

*with the **breastplate of righteousness** in place,*

The breastplate of righteousness guards your heart

If you plan to spend the rest of your life armoring up every day for the Glory of Christ, you have got to know your heart is going to get stomped on – **A LOT!!!**

> *[10] Blessed are those who are persecuted because of righteousness, for theirs is the kingdom of heaven.[11] "Blessed are you when people insult you, persecute you and falsely say all kinds of evil against you because of me. {Matthew 5:10-11 NIV}*

It is incredibly important that we come to the understanding early on in our relationship with God through Christ that it is a "HEART THING" not an "intellectual thing." Sadly, many people who call themselves Christians do not have nor do they enjoy the kind of personal – one on one – intimate – loving <u>heart</u> relationship with God that He longs to have with us.

Many people who say they are Christians are folks who at some point in their life have come to an "intellectual agreement" with a list religious and denominational practices that they think qualifies them at least in the eyes of their peers as being called Christian. When we allow that to happen to us, here's all we think a Christian needs to do to please God:

Most of us think that being a Christian means:

*Going to church on Sunday as often as we can {if not every Sunday at least on Easter and Christmas} and if were "REALLY GOOD" Christians we will go <u>every</u> Sunday and maybe even on Sunday night and Wednesday night.

*We know were supposed to give some money to the church when they run that plate by us every Sunday cause after all they've got to pay the light bill and stuff and the preacher needs something for his trouble.

*We're pretty sure we need to worship in a Christ-centered, Holy Ghost filled, Bible believing church where the pastor preaches fearlessly against sin and all the messages come directly from God's Word but more importantly we have to find a church that the shakers and movers attend, that has the fanciest facility, the most members, the most popular preacher, the biggest gym and fellowship hall and for sure the winningest church league soft ball and basket ball team.

*We should probably have at least one Bible that we can display conspicuously in our home so that friends who come over can "SEE" that we are Christians. Maybe we can even include a couple of crosses on the wall or a picture of Jesus just to enhance the appearance of a Christian home.

*We know that God expects us to spend some time in prayer and blessing especially when things aren't going well in our lives or occasionally when we sit down to a meal with other folks we think are Christians.

*We know that we shouldn't cuss or tell off-color jokes or take the Lord's name in vain but we all know God's got a sense of humor – <u>right</u>?

*We should try to be nice to other people and we do try to <u>as long as their nice to us.</u>

*We know we shouldn't lie or cheat or steal or gossip or slander or run around on our spouse or have sex before marriage or disrespect our parents or any of that stuff but "all have sinned and fallen short" right. That's why Christ had to die on the cross right – because people make mistakes - <u>they just can't help it.</u>

Maybe what you and I need to prove to all our friends and neighbors and co-workers that we REALLY ARE Christians is a "CHRISTIANITY KIT"

The Christianity Kit Would Contain These Items:

A Picture of Christ

A Fish Emblem

A Jesus Car Tag or Bumper Sticker

A Christian T-shirt

A Necklace with a Cross on it

A Huge Bible to put on our Coffee Table in the living room

A "As for me and my house" Door Mat

A Church Cook Book with one of our Recipes in it

A Certificate of Baptism

A Letter of Membership

A Perfect Attendance Pin

A Document Showing That We Are a Leader in our Church

Oh yeah, all these things are great and they may impress our friends, BUT, until we have FIRST met "GOD'S DEFINITION OF SALVATION" by receiving His Son Christ Jesus as our personal Lord and Savior …AND THEN… are TRULY "BEARING THE FRUIT" OF THAT RELATIONSHIP DAILY…

ALL THAT OTHER STUFF… DON'T MEAN DIDLEY SQUAT!!!

[14] …"*These are the words of the Amen, the faithful and true witness, the ruler of God's creation.* [15] *I know your deeds, that you are neither cold nor hot. I wish you were either one or the other!* [16] *So, because you are lukewarm—neither hot nor cold—I am about to spit you out of my mouth.* [17] *YOU SAY, 'I am rich; I have acquired wealth and do not need a thing.' BUT you do not realize that you are*

wretched, pitiful, poor, blind and naked. {Revelation 3:14-17}

And then this*: But you, man of God, flee from all this, **and pursue righteousness**, godliness, faith, love, endurance and gentleness. [12] Fight the good fight of the faith. Take hold of the eternal life to which you were called when you made your good confession in the presence of many witnesses. {1Timothy 6:11-12 NIV}*

Weapon Number Three

[15] and with your feet fitted with the readiness that comes from the gospel of peace.

Christ has called us all who love Him to one particularly important task. He lays it out clearly for us in

Matthew 28:18-20 NIV [18] Then Jesus came to them and said, "All authority in heaven and on earth has been given to me. [19] Therefore go and make disciples of all nations, baptizing them in the name of the Father and of the Son and of the Holy Spirit, [20] and teaching them to obey everything I have commanded you. And surely I am with you always, to the very end of the age."

Most country folks understand that when it's "Harvest Time" that doesn't mean that everybody goes and sits in the barn till the harvest shows up there. They fully understand that it means it's time to roll their sleeves up, get out in the harvest field and bring the harvest INTO the barn.

Why then do we think that the way to answer "the Great Commission" of Christ is to go plop our butts down in the church and let the "lost" come to us. True Christians understand that "yes" it's important to gather for worship in a central location regularly to encourage and prepare each other for the life challenges ahead, BUT the most effective ministering we can do for the glory of God will be as Luke 14:23 NIV says:

²³ "Then the master told his servant, 'Go out to the roads and country lanes and compel them to come in, so that my house will be full.

And in Matthew 9:36-38 (NIV)

³⁶ When he saw the crowds, he had compassion on them, because they were harassed and helpless, like sheep without a shepherd. ³⁷ Then he said to his disciples, "The harvest is plentiful but the workers are few. ³⁸ Ask the Lord of the harvest, therefore, to send out workers into his harvest field. "

Having your feet fitted with the readiness that comes from the Gospel of Peace will require a few important things from you. **First** - you will not just need to be in your Word – **you will need for the Word to be in you**; and that will require a hunger on your part to be in the Word of God every day – not just reading it – but studying it – absorbing it – understanding it – practicing it – applying it and praying for revelation knowledge from it. You cannot be effective in sharing the truth of God with others if you are not walking in that same truth for yourself.

And **second** you must receive, understand and apply these powerful scriptures pertaining to ministering to others given us in :{ Revelation 12:10-12 NIV}

¹⁰ Then I heard a loud voice in heaven say:

"Now have come the salvation and the power and the kingdom of our God,

and the authority of his Messiah.

For the accuser of our brothers and sisters,

who accuses them before our God day and night,
has been hurled down.
[11] They triumphed over him
by the blood of the Lamb
and by the word of their testimony;
they did not love their lives so much
as to shrink from death.
[12] Therefore rejoice, you heavens
and you who dwell in them!
But woe to the earth and the sea,
because the devil has gone down to you!
He is filled with fury,
because he knows that his time is short."

First the bad news: I have confessed many times over the last twenty years during a sermon that the "Pulpit Ministry" is the weakest and most ineffective ministry on the planet. Why have I reached that conclusion? Because every Sunday in Pulpits all over the United States of America, dedicated and sincere men and women stand before congregations of dozens or hundreds or thousands or tens of thousands preaching their hearts out concerning God's teachings on how we should live our lives and then we all leave our church, get in our cars, go home, disregard everything we've heard and go on living our daily lives directly opposite to what God's Word teaches. BUT here's the good news: I have discovered by experience through those same twenty years that there is no more powerful ministry on earth than the ministry of "personal testimony."

That's right – the most powerful and effective ministry is when one man or woman that has BEEN DELIVERED by Jesus Christ from their own hopelessness can reach across the table over a cup of coffee – take another broken and hurting man or woman's hand – wipe the tears pouring down their face and begin to give THEM the same LIVING HOPE someone once gave you. That's why the scriptures above remind us that there are two things in all of creation that are guaranteed to defeat the things of Hell – the combination of the Blood of Christ and our personal testimony.

1 Corinthians 10:13 NIV tells us that: [13] "No temptation has overtaken you except what is common to man."

That means that you are not the only person on the planet that has been as "jacked up" as you were {although Satan will try to convince you that you are}. Believe me when I say {because I am living it every day} – There is no one who can minister more effectively to someone who IS PRESENTLY "jacked up" than someone who HAS BEEN "jacked up." And there is NO ONE who can convince someone else that they can be delivered from their "jacked up" life by Jesus Christ like someone who ALREADY HAS. I'm telling you God just loves to take the worst possible situations and restore them in a way that makes the rest of the world shake their heads in wonderment. Check this scripture out:

[26] Brothers and sisters, think of what you were when you were called. Not many of you were wise by human standards; not many were influential; not many were of noble birth. [27] But God chose the foolish things of the world to shame the wise; God chose the weak things of the world to shame the strong. [28] God chose the lowly things of this world and the despised things—and the things that are not—to nullify the things that are, [29] so that no one may boast before him.{1Corinthians 1:26-29 NIV}

Weapon Number Four

[16] In addition to all this, take up the shield of faith, with which you can extinguish all the flaming arrows of the evil one.

I remember so well, though it was long ago, when God first showed me "by His Spirit "what this verse means.

I was studying these very scriptures at my desk one night and suddenly God seemed to make the phrase "flaming arrows of the evil one" lift off the page. That night I was reading out of the NIV Life Application Bible my sister-in-law had given me as a gift. {It was my first Bible} But, suddenly I heard the voice of God in my spirit saying: "Go find a King James Bible and see how it puts this same phrase." So I rose and started looking around the house for a King James Translation and there on a shelf nearby was my son's King James. So I pulled it down – turned to the scriptures and looked to see what it said. Instead of "flaming arrows" IT said "fiery darts." And I said, OK Lord, what about it?

And He said, now get up – go get a Concordance – and see what the Greek words for "fiery darts" are as used in this verse and how they are translated. Got up – got the Concordance – turned to the word "fiery." The Greek word for "fiery" was "puroo" which translated means "inflamed with anger, grief or lust." The Greek word for "darts" was "ballo" which translated means "to throw with violence or intensity."

Ok, so you are saying that I need the Shield of Faith because Satan is going to try to take me out by throwing flaming darts at me violently and intensely? Then He showed me a vision which fully answered the question. He showed me a huge room. And in the center of this room was a long table. And on the table were all kinds of bows for hunting – long bows, short bows, compound bows and cross bows. And beside them on the table were stacks of arrows. And the tips of each arrow was wrapped sackcloth. All around the room from floor to ceiling were shelves and on the shelves were what looked like one gallon paint buckets – except each bucket had a name written on it – HATRED, BIGOTRY, PREJUDICE, ANGER, REBELLION, LYING, DECEIPT, JEALOUSY, GREED, GOSSIP, ARROGANCE, PRIDE, LUST and many, many more. And then God said: "You see my son, Satan knows your weaknesses – he knows what button to push and he knows how to take you out.

He knows that some of your weaknesses have been sexual perversion, addiction to pornography and continuous infidelity. So, without your "shield of faith" he can simply take down a can of "LUST" off the shelf – dip the cloth tip of the arrow in it – set it on fire – place it in the bow of his choice and "LIGHT YOU UP!!!"

My experience is that God gives us the weapon of the Shield of Faith at the same time He gives all the others – but – over the years as you experience Him in your life day after day your shield begins to grow larger and larger giving you more and more protection from the wiles of Satan. Does he still try to shoot his fiery darts at me every once in a while. Yes he does BUT my friend there is no sweeter sound and nothing brings a bigger smile on my face than the recognizable sound of <u>HIS ARROWS</u> bouncing off of <u>MY BIG OLD SHIELD.</u>

You better get the shield – 'cause he's got your bucket...

Weapon Number Five

¹⁷ Take the helmet of salvation and...

The Helmet of Salvation is the weapon given to protect your mind. Joyce Meyer has written a bestselling book called: "The Battlefield of the Mind" There is not a much better way of pointing out the dangers of walking around without your Spiritual Helmet than that book title. If your heart is where your relationship with God takes place {and it is} then your mind is the devils playground. It is in your mind that he will try to pedal his lies, his temptations and his abominations. Without the combination of the weapons of the Breastplate of Righteousness and the Helmet of Salvation, he can even begin to harden your heart over time and rob you of the meaningful relationship that God wants to have with you. It's important to understand that putting on the mind protecting Helmet of Salvation comes only on the heels of <u>experiencing the act of Salvation</u>. God has clearly shown us the path to that life changing process:

⁸ But what does it say? "The word is near you; it is in your mouth and in your heart," that is, the message concerning the faith that we proclaim: ⁹ If you declare with your mouth, "Jesus is Lord," and believe in your heart that God raised him from the dead, you will be saved. ¹⁰ For it is with your heart that you believe and are justified, and it is with your mouth that you profess your faith and are saved.
{Romans 10:8-10 NIV}

I think it is critically important that we understand that while we are stating our confession that "Jesus is Lord" and our belief that God raised Christ from the dead, we need to fully understand several very important Kingdom facts.

FIRST, we need to make sure we understand what kind of covenant promise we are making Him if we truly want Him to become "Lord" of our life. Webster's Dictionary clearly defines for us what a "LORD" is.

Definition of "Lord": one who has complete authority, control, or power over others.

In other words you are pledging that you are giving yourself to Him a Romans 12:1-3 NIV commands:

12 Therefore, I urge you, brothers and sisters, in view of God's mercy, to offer your bodies as a living sacrifice, holy and pleasing to God—this is your true and proper worship. ² Do not conform to the pattern of this world, but be transformed by the renewing of your mind. Then you will be able to test and approve what God's will is—his good, pleasing and perfect will.

SECOND, we must understand that following Christ is no bed of roses. Luke 9:23 says

Then he said to them all: "Whoever wants to be my disciple must deny themselves and take up their cross daily and follow me.

And in Luke 9:58 NIV

⁵⁸ Jesus replied, "Foxes have dens and birds have nests, but the Son of Man has no place to lay his head."

THIRD, we must understand that receiving Christ as Lord and Master of our lives is not some instantaneous process whereby all our troubles fade away – the flowers burst into bloom –the sun leaps from behind the dark clouds of our past and the Bluebirds start singing – and everything is right with the world. Christ did not come into this world and suffer and die on the Cross of Calvary to make things better. On the contrary, He came because He knew things were not going to get any better. He didn't come to "protect the righteous." On the contrary He came to "save the sinner." That is why Philippians 2:12-16 NIV says:

¹² Therefore, my dear friends, as you have always obeyed— not only in my presence, but now much more in my absence—continue to work out your salvation with fear and trembling, ¹³ for it is God who works in you to will and to act in order to fulfill his good purpose.

¹⁴ Do everything without grumbling or arguing, ¹⁵ so that you may become blameless and pure, "children of God without fault in a warped and crooked generation." Then you will shine among them like stars in the sky ¹⁶ as you hold firmly to the word of life.

Put on the Helmet of Salvation. And once you have that weapon firmly in place all your "defensive" spiritual armor is now complete. Why do I say that, because the first five pieces of armor God gives you are the ones that will quickly protect your heart, mind, soul and spirit from the "slings and arrows" of the evil one while you continue to prepare to engage the enemy with the two "offensive" weapons God is about to give you. And the first "offensive weapon is…

Weapon Number Six

{your first offensive weapon}

The Sword of the Spirit, which is the Word of God.

There is no greater weapon that has ever been given to those who have come to fight in the Army of God than the Sword of the Spirit {the Word}.

*Hebrews 4:12 NIV [12] for the **Word of God** is alive and active. Sharper than any double-edged sword, it penetrates even to dividing soul and spirit, joints and marrow; it judges the thoughts and attitudes of the heart.*

*Proverbs 18:21 NIV [21] **Words** have the power of life and death, and those who love them will eat their fruit.*

*Deuteronomy 11:18-21 NIV [18] Fix these **Words** of mine in your hearts and minds; tie them as symbols on your hands and bind them on your foreheads. [19] Teach them to your children, talking about them when you sit at home and when you walk along the road, when you lie down and when you get up. [20] Write them on the doorframes of your houses and on your gates, [21] so that your days and the days of your children may be many in the land the Lord swore to give your ancestors.*

There is an old saying that says: "Sticks and stones will break will break my bones but "words" will never hurt me. That is a ball faced – low down – dirty lie. A single word has the absolute power to break more hearts, minds, souls and spirits than all the sticks and stones in this world combined. Some civilizations even believed that once spoken - words had "life" - a life that had no end. One form of that "life" we call GOSSIP. And we all know that a few negative, juicy words strung together by someone who wants to spread some bad news about somebody or something can take on a life of their own and with each passing day become more negative and more juicy.

Isaiah 40:8 (NIV) reminds us that:

> [8] *The grass withers and the flowers fall, but the Word of our God endures forever."*

I think of all the time I wasted in my old life chasing after the so-called advice of mortal men. I was constantly searching for and reading the latest self help books on the shelf to find that miraculous answer to all my problems. Books like:

*How to Win Friends and Influence People

*Keys to Success

*The Seven Habits of Highly Effective People

*How to Stop Worrying and Start Living

*When Bad Things Happen to Good People

*Games People Play

*Co-dependent No More

*Men are from Mars Women are from Venus

*And on and on and on.....

Oh, they were all great reads and very entertaining but now I know that there was already and had always been a Book that had offered up the exact same advice {and even more} before those books were ever written. It was just one Book but it had two sections, 66 books in one, 1189 chapters, over 31,000 verses and the absolute best advice on how to live life that has ever been written – PERIOD! It wasn't a book that you picked up and read and threw in the closet because you got all you could get out of it. On the contrary, it was the Book that was authored by the one individual that knew more about the thoughts and behaviors of mankind than anyone ever had or ever would.

WHY? Because He created us, He has been observing our behaviors and the consequences they have created literally since the beginning of time and He knows how to release us from those consequences and set us free.

That Book is the inerrant Word of God. It never grows old or out dated because human behavior does not change and the Word of God is "living and active." It changes with and grows with you throughout your life as you mature in your relationship with God to meet your present need. Nobody used the Word of God more effectively in Spiritual Warfare than Jesus Christ. There are many powerful examples in the Bible concerning Christ using God's Word to rebuke evil but I guess one of my favorites is when He used God's Word to shut down Satan during the "temptation in the desert."

4 Then Jesus was led by the Spirit into the wilderness to be tempted by the devil. ² After fasting forty days and forty nights, he was hungry. ³ The tempter came to him and said, "If you are the Son of God, tell these stones to become bread."

⁴ Jesus answered, "It is written: 'Man shall not live on bread alone, but on every word that comes from the mouth of God.'"

⁵ Then the devil took him to the holy city and had him stand on the highest point of the temple. ⁶ "If you are the Son of God," he said, "throw yourself down. For it is written:

"'He will command his angels concerning you, and they will lift you up in their hands, so that you will not strike your foot against a stone.'"

⁷ Jesus answered him, "It is also written: 'Do not put the Lord your God to the test.'"

⁸ Again, the devil took him to a very high mountain and showed him all the kingdoms of the world and their splendor. ⁹ "All this I will give you," he said, "if you will bow down and worship me."

¹⁰ Jesus said to him, "Away from me, Satan! For it is written: 'Worship the Lord your God, and serve him only.'"

¹¹ Then the devil left him, and angels came and attended him. {Matthew 4:1-11 NIV}

God calls His Word a SWORD. I can go to a store and I can buy myself a big, long, sharp, shiny sword. I can strap it on, hold my shoulders back and walk around in front of people with it. Those people make look at each other and say: WOW! He must be a swordsman. But if I haven't taken it out of the scabbard every day and become proficient in the use of it –I AIN'T no swordsman and if I have to use it in a life and death battle – I am going to be chopped liver. Carrying around the Sword of the Spirit {which is the Word of God} will work in your life the same way. If you don't spend time practicing your Biblical skills, you will have no offensive weapon that you can use effectively when drawn into mortal combat with the forces in the spirit realm that are coming to destroy you. If you don't take out the Word of God daily to read it, study it and apply it to your life you AIN'T no real soldier in the Army of God and Satan will carve you up like a Thanksgiving Turkey.

Weapon Number Seven

{your second offensive weapon}

[18] And pray <u>in the Spirit</u> on all occasions with all kinds of prayers and requests. With this in mind, be alert and always keep on praying for all the Lord's people.

Learn to combine the "Sword of the Spirit" with "Praying in the Spirit" and you will have the only two weapons you will ever need to bring the enemy to his knees.

James 5:13-16 NIV validates that statement when it boldly states:

[13] Is anyone among you in trouble? Let them pray. Is anyone happy? Let them sing songs of praise. [14] Is anyone among you sick? Let them call the elders of the church to pray over them and anoint them with oil in the name of the Lord. [15] And the prayer offered in faith will make the sick person well; the Lord will raise them up. If they have sinned, they will be forgiven. [16] Therefore confess your sins to each other and pray for each other so that you may be healed. ***The prayer of a righteous person is powerful and effective.***

Ok, so what does "praying in the Spirit "mean?

Praying in the Spirit can have several different meanings. It can mean "by means of," "with the help of," "in the sphere of" or "in connection to" the Spirit. Praying in the Spirit does not refer to the words we are saying. Rather, it refers to <u>how</u> we are praying. Praying in the Spirit is praying according to the <u>Spirit's leading</u>. It is praying for things that the <u>Spirit</u> leads us to pray for. When you are praying what the Spirit is leading you to pray for, you will find yourself praying for the things <u>God </u>wants for you instead of praying for what <u>you want for yourself.</u> Believe me when I tell you that you will be much happier receiving what God wants for you than what you have always selfishly wanted for yourself.

The weapon of "praying in the Spirit" much like the "Sword of the Spirit" requires consistent daily practice with the weapon if you are to be effective with it in your daily battles. The prayer of a soldier in the Army of God is not a quick little daily recitation like:

"Now I lay me down to sleep.
I pray the Lord my soul to keep.
Amen"
OR
"God is good.
God is great.
Thank you for the food we ate. Amen"

Praying in the Spirit is a deeply personal, private, soul searching intimate time with the God of all creation and should always be approached with the respect and humility that go with understanding that.

One day Jesus was praying in a certain place. When he finished, one of his disciples said to him, "Lord, teach us to pray, just as John taught his disciples."{Luke 11:1 NIV}

If we can understand His answer, we will have a powerful prayer life. His answer came in the form of what you and I refer to as the "Lord's Prayer" given in Matthew 6:9-13. Although those scriptures too have become a recitation, that was never Christ's intention how it should be used. He makes that clear at the very beginning in Verse 9 when He says:

9 "This, then, is <u>how</u> you should pray:
{Not when, where or who - HOW}

"'Our Father in heaven,

This verse cautions us to stop and consider as we enter into a time of prayer just WHO it is we are addressing – "the Creator of all things in Heaven and Earth." It is a gentle reminder that HE is GOD and we ain't.

hallowed be your name,

This verse prompts us to spend some time in the beginning of this special moment with HIM to praise His Name before we launch into our personal complaints and needs as so many of us selfishly do <u>if</u> and when we pray. I want Him to know in those early moments with Him that I know full well who He is and that I am humbled by that knowledge. He is Yaweh. He is Jehovah. He is the God of Abraham, Isaac and Jacob. He is the Alpha and the Omega. He is the God and Father of my Lord and Savior Jesus Christ. He is my full portion. He is my all in all. He is the breath I am breathing. He is every beat of my heart. He is the soundness of my mind, the health of my body and the strength of my bones – and I want Him to know that I know that right up front.

10 your kingdom come,

This verse prompts us to declare and affirm to Him continuously that we know we are "Kingdom Citizens" and no longer citizens of this world and that we pledge allegiance to God not man. It is important to me to confirm to Him that I know I am simply passing through this world to complete the destiny and purpose that He brought me to this earth to complete and that I know that when it has been accomplished He will bring me home to be with Him for eternity.

your will be done,

This verse reminds us of the importance of acknowledging to God that we understand that HIS "love language" is "acts of obedience." That is why He tells us straight forwardly in His Word – "if you love Me, you will obey My commands" and in another place He tells us that to Him – "obedience is more important than sacrifice."

on earth as it is in heaven.

The Book of Ephesians tells us in Chapter 1 that "God has blessed us in the Heavenly realms with every Spiritual blessing in Christ." When we ask God to let His Kingdom come and His will be done {on earth as it is in Heaven} we are confessing and acknowledging to Him that in faith we believe that promise. And that we further believe that as

"Kingdom Citizens" we should boldly claim those blessing in our life while we are here on earth.

[11] Give us today our daily bread.

Well, what do you know? We have finally come to the place in Christ's teaching about <u>HOW</u> we should pray where He tells us: "<u>NOW</u> is the time folks where you can begin what you normally jump into when you pray from the "git go" and that is telling God what YOU want and what YOU need.

Matthew 6:8 tells us that; *"our Father in Heaven knows what we need before we ask Him."*

Then why do we need to ask Him you say?

This is how God helped me understand the answer to that question. I have three beautiful daughters who are all grown up now BUT I remember when they were much younger. And one Christmas I happened to walk into one of their rooms and saw a hand written note to Santa lying beside one of their beds.

I picked up the note and glanced at it and it said: "Dear Santa, would you please give me a Barbie Bicycle for Christmas." I put the note down and knowing in my heart what she wanted, I purposed in my heart she would receive it. But the most joyous moment was when later that day she came into the living room – climbed up into my lap - rolled those beautiful little eyes and said: Daddy, would you get me a Barbie Bicycle for Christmas. What a precious moment for a loving father to be able to share with His child. You see God loves those special moments as well. He's heard you confess your needs out loud but it's when you come to Him – one on one – and in the Spirit realm climb up in his lap in a moment of private prayer and tell him what you need that most delights Him.

¹² And forgive us our debts,

This verse is a reminder that we should never rise from our time with God in prayer that we do not readily confess and ask forgiveness for our failures in daily life as it relates to His expectations.

as we also have forgiven our debtors.

And that we further acknowledge to him that because of His unconditional love, mercy and forgiveness poured out on us in spite of our sins –WE should also be quick to offer that same grace to those who have sinned against us.

¹³ And lead us not into temptation,

This verse reminds us that we were born of a sin nature and therefore have a natural propensity to succumb to temptation which leads to sin in our lives. It is important that continuously ask God in prayer to strengthen us against temptation. He promises us in **1 Corinthians 10:13** that:

{*"No temptation has overtaken you except what is common to mankind. And God is faithful; he will not let you be tempted beyond what you can bear. But when you are tempted, he will also provide a way out so that you can endure it."}*

Therefore pray for him to give you the strength to "bear each temptation" and when temptation suddenly traps you - to show you the "way out of it."

but deliver us from the evil one.

Always take time in prayer to confess and confirm that you understand that the devil will always looking for an opportune time to take you out. Satan loves to attack you during times of worry or anxiety or fear or anger. Remember and acknowledge to God that you know that HE is your shield. He is your strong tower. He is your deliverer. The battles and the victories will be fought and won for His glory, not yours or mine.

Because, as the final verse of this prayer lesson plainly states:

*"**HE** is the Kingdom and the Power and the Glory forever – AMEN!!!"*

Congratulations you have been officially "Armored Up"

And <u>HERE</u> is where you are in "The Journey"

FIRST - You have to be submitted to the will of God and dare to walk with Him through the Valley of Bones. There, you must take complete responsibility for your past mistakes. You have to confess them. You must repent of them. You must accept the painful truth that you cannot go back and change them. <u>BUT,</u> you have learned in faith that the sins of your past do not define your Destiny. They are mistakes you have made – they are not who you are. Armed with that truth, you have now reached the point that you can believe "in Faith" that God has forgiven you those things through the shed blood of His Son Christ Jesus and so you have received that forgiveness and are free from the shame of your past. You have made up your mind once and for all that you will NOT look back over your shoulder again but rather, you will put your shoulders back – lift your head high and fix your eyes only on your future in Christ.

SECOND – You have been thoroughly instructed in: the reason for, the power of, and the proper implementation and use of "The Armor of God." Understanding the importance of each weapon {whether defensive or offensive} and in obedience to God's instruction you have put on the FULL ARMOR – and have taken YOUR STAND – <u>FIRMLY</u>:

Belt of Truth – CHECK
Breastplate of Righteousness – CHECK
Feet Fitted with the Readiness of the Gospel – CHECK
Shield of Faith – CHECK
Helmet of Salvation – CHECK
Sword of the Spirit {the Word} – CHECK
Spirit Prayer – CHECK

SO NOW THE TIME HAS COME FOR YOU TO
RECEIVE:

PART FIVE

THE KEYS TO VICTORIOUS LIVING

SO LET'S GET STARTED

In late 1996, about six months after I had taken Christ as my personal Lord and Savior, I came under the leading of a great man of God. His name is Pastor Jack Giles – founder and long time Pastor of Church of the Way in Meridian, Mississippi. He recognized my calling and he encouraged me, mentored me, and helped direct me to my destiny. For that time with him I will remain eternally grateful. One Sunday morning he came to me and said:

"Brother Charlie, we are going to have our annual men's retreat in a couple of weeks at a local lake resort. All the men of Church of the Way will be there together in fellowship and worship. I was just wondering if you would like to lead one of our evening devotions."

Well, that was a big stack of "good news" and "bad news" at the same time. The "good news" was that I knew God was calling me to teach His Word to the broken and hurting and hopeless and here was a chance for me to get started. But, the "bad news" was I didn't feel like I had spent near enough time in the Bible yet to consider myself qualified or competent to teach ANYBODY from it. Today I know full well that the "good news" was coming from God and the "bad news" was coming from Satan. I have founded and operated three VERY successful Christ centered addiction recovery centers over the last 20 years and I have read the Bible through NUMEROUS times and preached thousands of sermons on radio, television and the internet – and you know what – I'm still not qualified to do it but – BUT Jesus Christ who is "in me" – He is the one who qualifies me to do it.

So, with the devotion challenge before me and the Holy Spirit in me I began to fervently pray that God would lead me to the scriptures He wanted me to teach from – and He did. He reminded me of a story I once read in a Children's Bible Story Book - you know, the kind with the BIG pages and BIG print and BIG color pictures depicting a scene from the bible story you were reading.

He brought back to my remembrance the picture in the book of a young shepherd boy wearing nothing but sandals and a loin cloth – holding a sling shot in his hand. In the picture he was facing a giant man {armored from head to toe} with a giant sword in his hand. I remembered that it was the story of David and Goliath. I felt God prompting me that these were the scriptures He wanted me to use to preach what turned out to be – my VERY FIRST sermon. I was too new in my relationship with God and to immature in His Word in those early days to understand that He was not just showing me some quick scriptures for devotion, but He was leading me to a group of scriptures that I would read hundreds of times. He was leading me to a group of scriptures that I would teach hundreds of times. He was leading me to a group of scriptures that would teach me hundreds of times about living a victorious life. And He was leading me to a group of scriptures that have helped thousands of broken, hopeless, hurting people to gain victory in their lives.

Now let me share these awesome scriptures with you so that you may also have

"The Keys to Victorious Living."

We are going to start in

1 Samuel 17 Verse 1 {NIV}

Now the Philistines {the enemy} gathered their forces for war and assembled at Sokoh in Judah. They pitched camp at Ephes Dammim, between Sokoh and Azekah. ² Saul and the Israelites {God's chosen people} assembled and camped in the Valley of Elah and drew up their battle line to meet the Philistines.

Key Number 1

***You and I MUST come to understand that the Enemy – Satan and his imps are now - always have been and always will be "gathered for war."**

Their sole purpose 24/7 is to remain fired up about and absolutely committed to completely annihilating you, your family, your relationships, your character, your career, your future AND your relationship with God. That is why the Word of God warns us in 2 Peter to:

"Be self controlled and alert. Because, your enemy the devil prowls around like a roaring lion looking for someone to devour."

BUT what do these verses say God's chosen people are doing – Gathering for war? Oh no! THEY are **"assembled and camped."** Listen to me. Soldiers gather their forces for war! <u>BOY SCOUTS</u> assemble and camp {and cook flap jacks and sing around the camp fire}. The first thing we <u>MUST</u> do if we are going to live a victorious life is to understand that we are not Boy Scouts. We must be a well trained, fully armored and prepared Spiritual Force - understanding that we are constantly in a warfare situation if we are going to serve in the Army of God. We cannot afford to let our Spiritual guard down <u>EVER.</u> Please don't misunderstand me. Church definitely has its place in a Soldier of God's life. It is a place where he can go to be encouraged by and lifted up by his fellow soldiers. But too many times we are getting too comfortable at "church" and letting it become a Boy Scout Jamboree. And suddenly, we find ourselves getting so comfortable "flipping spiritual flap jacks and singing spiritual songs around the campfire" that we forget we were called to be Soldiers and the War we are in must take place <u>outside</u> of the "spiritual bunker" and <u>on the Battle Field</u>.

If we are going to be victorious, let's rise up - walk to the front lines and "get it on." God has fully prepared us.

[3] *The Philistines {evil} occupied one hill and the Israelites {goodness} another, with the valley between them.*

Key Number 2

***I have learned that in order to live a "Victorious Life" we must understand that we will forever be faced with the fact that life will always be comprised of "two hills with a valley in between."

Two hills – one named Evil and the other Good – one named Damnation and the other Salvation – one named Slave Master and the other Lord and Master – one named Disgrace and the other Honor – one named Defeat and the other Victory. But only in The Valley will the answer be found as to which "hill" prevails. And the righteousness of God will only prevail in this world, this Nation, this State, this County, this City or this Town when a Soldier of God is willing to walk down off the comfort of <u>HIS</u> hill and meet the enemy confidently waiting for him in The Valley.

[4] A champion named Goliath, who was from Gath, came out of the Philistine camp. His height was six cubits and a span.

He seemed insurmountable…

[5] He had a bronze helmet on his head and wore a coat of scale armor of bronze weighing five thousand shekels; [6] on his legs he wore bronze greaves, and a bronze javelin was slung on his back.

He seemed impenetrable…

[7] His spear shaft was like a weaver's rod, and its iron point weighed six hundred shekels. His shield bearer went ahead of him.

He seemed undefeatable…

Key Number 3

***To be Victorious in life we must be ready to accept and prepare for the fact that we will all have to face "Goliaths" in our life.

I'm not talking about the little daily inconveniences and aggravations that are always around. I'm talking about the "Goliaths" – those problems that come against us in life that can destroy us emotionally, physically, mentally and Spiritually – things like the death of a loved one, divorce, loss of your job, bankruptcy, a serious illness, prejudice, bigotry, anger, rebellion, un-forgiveness, alcoholism, drug addiction or imprisonment – "GIANT SIZED" PROBLEMS. Here's the "bad news." When those things confront you they <u>SEEM</u> insurmountable, impenetrable, and undefeatable. Here's the "good news." You <u>CAN defeat</u> them but you will have to have the courage to walk down off the comfort of your "hill" and meet the enemy head on in the valley.

[8] *Goliath stood and shouted to the ranks of Israel, "Why do you come out and line up for battle? Am I not a Philistine, and are you not the servants of Saul? Choose a man and have him come down to me.* [9] *If he is able to fight and kill me, we will become your subjects; but if I overcome him and kill him, you will become our subjects and serve us."*

Key Number 4

***Those life changing problems will come to you every morning and take their stand just like Goliath and declare to you your hopeless situation:

"Why do you come out and line up for battle? Am I not DIVORCE and are you not the poor sucker losing your marriage. Don't you know how many families I have ripped apart? You better stay up there on that hill boy.

"Hey, why do you come out and line up for battle? Am I not crack cocaine, heroine and crystal meth all rolled up in to one. Don't you know how many lives I have destroyed – how many people I have sent to prison – and you think YOU are going to defeat me? Ha Ha Ha! You better get back on that that hill full of losers boy."

Listen to me!

Goliath was a "Bully." A giant man standing in the valley running off at the mouth – stomping his feet - kicking up a bunch of dust and making a bunch of threats he wasn't going to be able to carry out – because what he didn't realize in this moment of arrogance was that he was already defeated – he just didn't know it yet. HEAR ME! If you are going to overcome the "Goliaths" in your life, you must understand THIS biblical truth: SATAN is a "Bully." He loves to get up in your face – intimidate you – threaten you – lie to you and double dog dare you to come meet him in battle because in his arrogance he refuses to realize that he is already defeated as well. He was defeated at the Cross of Calvary. He has no authority over the life of a true Soldier of God.

[10] *Then the Philistine {**the enemy**} said, "This day I defy the armies of Israel {**of God Almighty**}! Give me a man and let us fight each other."* *[11]* *On hearing the Philistine's words, Saul and all the Israelites {**God's chosen people**} were **dismayed** and **terrified.***

Key Number 5

***A fully forgiven – armored up – spiritually prepared Soldier in the Army of God is <u>NEVER</u> dismayed or terrified – vigilant, cautious, discerning, curious, inquisitive, expectant or observant – YES – dismayed or terrified - NO!

When a professional fighter steps into the ring to face an incredibly formidable opponent he is neither dismayed nor terrified. Why, because he knows that he is personally trained and ready for the battle and he does not under estimate the strength, prowess or intent of his opponent. More importantly he has carefully studied his opponent's methods of fighting <u>prior to</u> the battle and he is fully prepared to defend himself from those methods. When the fight begins and his opponent lands a painful and effective shot to his body – he doesn't run to the referee and cry: "Hey no fair, that guy just hit me." He knows that one of the risks of entering the battle is that you might get wounded somewhere in the process. Soldiers in the Army of God wake up every morning – strap on the armor and walk to the front lines to fight the "good fight of Faith" knowing full well that they may come back wounded or not come back at all. BUT they rise every day of their lives to do it anyway for the Glory of God.

Why? Because God's Word tells us that He does not give us a "spirit of fear."

He tells us: "We will not fear the terror of night, nor the arrow that flies by day".

He also tells us that: "In all these things we are more than conquerors through him who loved us."

---

*¹² Now David was the son of an Ephrathite named Jesse, who was from Bethlehem in Judah. Jesse had eight sons, and in Saul's time he was very old. ¹³ **Jesse's three oldest sons had followed Saul to the war:** The firstborn was Eliab; the second, Abinadab; and the third, Shammah. ¹⁴ David was the youngest. The three oldest followed Saul, ¹⁵ but David went back and forth from Saul to tend his father's sheep at Bethlehem.*

¹⁶ For forty days the Philistine came forward every morning and evening and took his stand.

Key Number 6

***Just as is indicated in verse 16 above the giant sized problems that have found their way in to your life will be relentless...

Day after day – night after night – week after week – month after month – year after year {if not confronted and defeated} your problems will come forward to intimidate you and dare you to come down into the valley and fight. Finding yourself paralyzed with fear – sitting up on the hillside with your knees knocking, your teeth chattering, and the fear of failure binding you hand and foot will never solve the problem nor ever make the problem give up and walk away. On the contrary, your failure to act will only encourage the problem to intimidate you more aggressively.

You have everything to gain and nothing to lose when you find yourself in The Valley.

At the end of your rope there is ALWAYS hope in "The Valley."

[17] Now Jesse said to his son David, "Take this ephah of roasted grain and these ten loaves of bread for your brothers and hurry to their camp. [18] Take along these ten cheeses to the commander of their unit. See how your brothers are and bring back some assurance from them. ***[19] They are with Saul and all the men of Israel in the Valley of Elah, <u>fighting against the Philistines</u>.***"

Key Number 7

"Liar Liar – Pants on fire!" Saul and Army of God were NOT in the Valley "fighting against the Enemies of God." They were sitting up on their hill "dismayed and terrified."

***Oh, they had convinced those they left behind that's what they were doing AND sadly had convinced themselves that was what they were doing but they were lying to themselves and everyone else about what was really going on.**

 If David came out to the Valley on the promise of his father and his brothers that he was going to have a front row seat to witness a battle where the Army of God gains complete victory over the Enemies of God – he needs to go ask for a refund on his ticket – because he AIN'T going to see that battle.

Oh, David WILL get to see the enemy {in the form of the giant} come down into the Valley for the fortieth time in a row to dare and intimidate the Army of God with his empty threats: "HEY! Come on down her you "yellow bellies" and I will cut you up like an anchovy…"

You and I MUST bring ourselves to understand that just talking about what we are going to do about the problems we face in life but not lifting a finger to do something about them will just allow them to become measurably worse day by day. You see, if someone did not take a stand against Goliath soon, he would have confirmed that he was indeed facing a bunch of cowards who had no appetite for battle and he would confidently begin to walk out of the valley – walk up THEIR hill and start whacking off some cowardly heads. Understand that that is exactly the way the Enemy operates in <u>YOUR</u> life. Left unchecked concerning his attacks on you, he will draw closer – become more confident in his ability to defeat you and take you into depths of despair you never dreamed of. Some of you reading this book know what I'm talking about because you have "been there".

*[20] Early in the morning David left the flock in the care of a shepherd, loaded up and set out, as Jesse had directed. **He reached the camp as the army was going out to its battle positions, <u>shouting the war cry.</u>***

You can bet that the "battle position" that that the Army of God was going out to "occupy" was no further than the bottom of their hill. They did not now possess nor would they ever possess the courage to become what I call **"Valley Men."** No, they were perfectly satisfied to go through life as **"Hill Men"** {more about that later} When we are faced in life with serious problems that have the power to destroy our lives and our future, just standing around "banging on your shield" and "shaking your fist" at the problem while "bragging loudly" about what your "gonna" do about it with no real intention of doing anything will kill you.

"I'M GONNA" AIN'T NEVER DID NOTHING!"

[21] Israel and the Philistines were drawing up their lines facing each other. [22] David left his things with the keeper of supplies, ran to the battle lines and asked his brothers how they were. [23] As he was talking with them, Goliath, the Philistine champion from Gath, stepped out from his lines and shouted his usual defiance,

Get Ready! Get Ready! Get Ready!

A "MAJOR TURN" in the events of this day are about to occur. WHY? Because in spite of all the "Hill Men" holding up the Victory for all this time: A "VALLEY MAN" IS ABOUT TO APPEAR...

You and I are getting ready to see firsthand what happens when a Soldier in the Army of God shows up. Because right here in the **last four words of Verse 23 -** *EVERYTHING CHANGES!*

Why? Because those four words say:

"*...and <u>David</u> heard it*".

If you and I can press in <u>right now</u> and examine the difference a "David" makes in what seems like an impossible situation under the control of what "looks like" an insurmountable, impenetrable and undefeatable foe, we will come out of this lesson with a life changing understanding of what you and I MUST <u>do,</u> <u>think,</u> <u>believe</u> and <u>initiate</u> in our lives to be able to have victory over all the things that will certainly come against us while we are on this earth.

[24] Whenever the Israelites saw the man, they all fled from him in great fear. [25] Now the Israelites had been saying, "Do you see how this man keeps coming out? He comes out to defy Israel. The king will give great wealth to the man who kills him. He will also give him his daughter in marriage and will exempt his family from taxes in Israel."

Key Number 8

***You will never know the joy of victory in your life if you are always making excuses about why you can't overcome your problems OR trying to bribe somebody else to solve your problems for you.

I spend MY life these days teaching men and women HOW they can war against those things that are trying to destroy them. But they will fail unless they understand that I am in that position because I understood that I was the one who had to fight my personal battles – no one could do it for me. That's why I often say to those I am ministering too: "I can walk this out WITH you but I cannot walk it out FOR you."

Now let's take a look at Verse 26 and begin to discover the "attitude" that David had about this sorry situation that makes HIM a Victorious Soldier in the Army of God instead of a Coward on the Hill.

*26 David asked the men standing near him, "What will be done for the man who kills this Philistine **and removes this disgrace from Israel? Who is this uncircumcised Philistine that he should defy the armies of the living God?"** 27 They repeated to him what they had been saying and told him, "This is what will be done for the man who kills him."*

Key Number 9

Let me give you the Pastor Charlie interpretation on this verse so you can better understand David's immediate reaction to and hostile attitude about the situation he was looking at. First of all, he is thinking – where in the heck is King Saul? Why in the world is he trying to pay somebody else to go down and fight the giant when he is obviously the most qualified man to be down in the Valley fighting him? And why isn't he down there already? What in "Sam Hill" are these thousands of God's people sitting on their sorry butts for up on this Hill for forty days listening to this "blow hard" calling them a bunch of "yellow bellies." And even worse, allowing him to curse our God.

***I don't know what these guys are gonna do BUT in the Name of Jehovah – I ain't puttin' up with this another minute.

28 When Eliab, David's oldest brother, heard him speaking with the men, he burned with anger at him and asked, "Why have you come down here? And with whom did you leave those few sheep in the wilderness? I know how conceited you are and how wicked your heart is; you came down only to watch the battle."

Key Number 10

I'm sure David is saying to himself – Yeah Bro, why don't you tell me when you guys are going to decide to actually get in the battle.

{But I digress} Key number 10 has to do with why Verse 28 exposes that Eliab{David's oldest brother} "burned with anger at him."

***There will always be those people in your life that <u>ought to be</u> setting a better example for you on how to live life victoriously like your dad or your grand dad or your boss or like in the case of David your older brother – but they aren't.

You see as the oldest brother, Eliab should have been showing David what a Spiritual Hero looks like – what an over-comer looks like – what a Victor looks like. But no, he was up on the Hill paralyzed with fear just like everyone else and David knew it. When those who should be setting the example for us in life fall short they often become angry when the less experienced person <u>THEY</u> should be mentoring is forced to set the right example for <u>THEM.</u> That is why Eliab is so angry. He is coming face to face with the fact that his "little brother" is schooling <u>HIM</u> on how to be a hero.

***People that refuse to take responsibility will always resent those who do.

When they show up in your family or circle of "so called friends" do not let it discourage you. Keep pressing in and keep setting the example.

²⁹ "Now what have I done?" said David. "Can't I even speak?" ³⁰ He then turned away to someone else and brought up the same matter, and the men answered him as before. ³¹ **What David said was overheard and reported to Saul, and Saul sent for him.**

It may sound impossible to you to believe but the truth is that a true Soldier in the Army of God {even if he is only a young shepherd boy} can teach a <u>KING</u> how to be a <u>MAN</u>.

So -

David said to Saul, "Let no one lose heart on account of this Philistine; your servant will go and fight him." **BUT -** *Saul replied, "You are not able to go out against this Philistine and fight him; you are only a young man, and he has been a warrior from his youth."*

Key Number 11

***Always beware of the "Nay Sayers "in your life.

You know, those people who don't have any desire to get off <u>THEIR</u> rear ends and accomplish or overcome anything but want to be the first in line to give you all the reasons <u>THEY THINK</u> you will never be able to accomplish anything worthwhile in life either.

*[34] But David said to Saul, "Your servant has been keeping his father's sheep. When a lion or a bear came and carried off a sheep from the flock, [35] I went after it struck it and rescued the sheep from its mouth. When it turned on me, I seized it by its hair, struck it and killed it. [36] Your servant has killed both the lion and the bear; this uncircumcised Philistine will be like one of them, because he has defied the armies of the living God. [37] **The Lord who rescued me from the paw of the lion and the paw of the bear will rescue me from the hand of this Philistine."***

Key Number 12

Come go with me as we discover one of the most powerful and revealing secrets on HOW to walk out your life in complete VICTORY. Verses 34 through 37 reveal to us the attitude, the understanding, the motivation, the beliefs and the actions that drive the heart of a Spiritual Warrior and Leader of Men.

First – all of David's young life he was walking out his Destiny <u>and he knew it</u>. David knew beyond a shadow of a doubt that he was in the center of God's will for his life. God called David to be a SHEPHERD and David said YES to that calling. In obedience to God he spent every day of his life caring for, leading, feeding and protecting the sheep. When a 10 foot tall Grizzly Bear or a ferocious roaring Lion came to carry off one of the sheep God had entrusted him with, he quickly came to its defense. But, <u>GET THIS</u>, because it is very important.

***At – <u>no time</u> did David ever go after the Lion or the Bear because he believed that he had the skills or the strength to defeat it. He went after them because he believed with all his heart that because God had called him to be a shepherd and shepherds were called to protect the flock – that the same God who called him to do it - <u>would also see him through it.</u>

Therein lies the courage and the strength that made David victorious - not just with the sheep - but throughout his life in Battle after Battle as a Soldier in the Army of God. He knew the minute he walked into the Valley of Elah and summed up the sorry situation before his eyes that he was standing in a divine moment – a calling from Almighty God. <u>He thought</u> he was coming to deliver some cheese and bread to the soldiers but now he realized that God was calling him <u>once again</u> to accomplish what seemed impossible for a mortal man but not impossible with God.

***ALL of us –YES EVEN YOU came into this world with a Destiny.

Sadly most of us never fully step into that Destiny because we were drawn away from it by the Evil One because of the needs of our flesh, the lust of our eyes, and the pride of life. That's why God warns us in Ephesians when he says:

"...it is by grace you have been saved, through faith—and this is not from yourselves, it is the gift of God— [9] *not by works, so that no one can boast."*

Saul said to David, "Go, and the Lord be with you." [38] *Then Saul dressed David in his own tunic. He put a coat of armor on him and a bronze helmet on his head.* [39] *David fastened on his sword over the tunic and tried walking around, because he was not used to them. "I cannot go in these," he said to Saul, <u>"because I am not used to them."</u> So he took them off.* [40] *Then he took his staff in his hand, chose five smooth stones from the stream, put them in the pouch of his shepherd's bag and, with his sling in his hand, approached the Philistine.*

Key Number 13

***Don't ever let someone else try to strap their armor on you and tell you how to fight <u>your</u> Spiritual Battles in life when they can't even fight their own.

David didn't need the fancy steel, brass and bonze armor of the king. He was used to fighting his battles {and winning them} with the Spiritual armor provided him by God Almighty – you remember – the belt, the breast plate, the feet fitted, the shield, the helmet, the sword and prayer – the spiritual weapons – not the weapons of man. David went to face the impossible with a smile in his heart because he was confident fighting this battle with what God had always provided. And with God's help, a simple sling a stone would do the job just fine.

[41] Meanwhile, the Philistine {the enemy}, with his shield bearer in front of him, kept coming closer to David. [42] He looked David over and saw that he was little more than a boy, glowing with health and handsome, and he despised him. [43] He said to David, "Am I a dog that you come at me with sticks?" And the Philistine cursed David by his gods. [44] "Come here," he said, "and I'll give your flesh to the birds and the wild animals!"

Key Number 14

***Understand that when you finally decide to turn from the fears of your past and walk down into the Valley - that evil thing that has invested so much of its time seeking to destroy you will be VERY unhappy that you have decided to come down and confront it. Those last moments of the confrontation will be the most challenging moments of your life because the enemy will recognize your strength and despise you for it.

He will get in your face. You will smell his foul breath in your nostrils. He will press in on you with a murderous look in his eyes. He will be filled with hate and he will curse you like a "yard dog" in one last futile effort to terrorize you and run you back up on the Hill with the rest of the cowards who are still sitting up there expecting to see you get fed to the birds and wild animals as promised. But suddenly that over confident Giant from the Army of Evil was about to hear someone say something to him that not only had he never heard but that he never imagined in his wildest nightmares he would ever hear another man say to him.

[45] David said to the Philistine, "You come against me with sword and spear and javelin, but I come against you in the name of the Lord Almighty, the God of the armies of Israel, whom you have defied. [46] This day the Lord will deliver you into my hands, and I'll strike you down and cut off your head. This very day I will give the carcasses of the Philistine army to the birds and the wild animals, and the whole world will know that there is a God in Israel. [47] All those gathered here will know that it is not by sword or spear that the Lord saves; for the battle is the Lord's, and he will give all of you into our hands."

Key Number 15

***WOW! Isn't it time that you and I have the courage to stand before the Goliath sized problems trying to destroy our lives and "in Faith" declare something similar?

Something like: No, let me tell <u>YOU</u> something "crack cocaine." Let me tell <u>YOU</u> something "Heroin." Let me tell <u>YOU</u> something "Alcohol." In Jesus name I declare that you will no longer have a hold on me – my life or my family. And I hereby rebuke any threats or temptations that you might try to use to pull me back into my old life.

No, let me tell YOU something Pornography, Bigotry, Rebellion, Anger, Infidelity Un-forgiveness and Divorce you are out of my life once and for all and forever in Jesus Name. Because I now know full well that my Father in Heaven has a plan and a purpose for my life – AND YOU AIN'T IN IT"

[48] *As the Philistine moved closer to attack him, <u>David ran quickly</u> toward the battle line to meet him.*

Key Number 16

If you have taken responsibility for your past – confessed it – repented of it – accepted the forgiveness of God for it – turned your back on it – armored up and set your eyes on your future in Christ – then it's time to come down off that Hill of Failure and take your stand in the Valley of Victorious Living. So what is stopping you? Why are you hesitating?

Get up RIGHT NOW and do a Hebrews 12:1

*12 Therefore, since we are surrounded by such a great cloud of witnesses, let us **throw off everything that hinders** and **the sin that so easily entangles**. And let us **run with perseverance the race marked out for us**, ² **fixing our eyes on Jesus**, the pioneer and perfecter of faith. {Who} For the joy set before him endured the cross, scorning its shame, and sat down at the right hand of the throne of God. ³ Consider him who endured such opposition from sinners, so that you will not grow weary and lose heart.*

⁴⁹ Reaching into his bag and taking out a stone, he slung it and struck the Philistine on the forehead. The stone sank into his forehead, and he fell face down on the ground. ⁵⁰ So David triumphed over the Philistine with a sling and a stone; without a sword in his hand he struck down the Philistine....

Key Number 17

***Learning to "walk out your faith" in victory as a Soldier of God involves a long process. It is <u>NOT</u> an overnight journey.

On the contrary it is the "Journey of a Lifetime." It's not a one shot victory. It must be a <u>CONFIRMED</u> <u>DEFEAT</u>. If you take the time to read the complete account of David's life in God's word, it will confirm in you that David was forced to fight battles his entire life. The ones where he was victorious were won in faith by the Hand of God. The ones that were lost were fought in his own strength reasoned out by his own intellect. That is why God reminds us in Philippians 2 that we must: "continue to work out our salvation with fear and trembling…" You must guard yourself carefully against launching in to a "PREMATURE CELEBRATION" of victory just because you ran down the hill into to the Valley and knocked the evil giant in your life down with a sling and a stone.

Let me see if I can explain the terms "Premature Celebration" and "Confirmed Defeat" this way: Let's say you decided to take a buddy of yours and go hunting for Grizzly Bears. Let's say you get out there in the woods and suddenly you run up on a twelve foot tall, mean, angry and hostile Grizzly running right at you full speed with his claws extended and his teeth gnashing. You quickly raise your gun and fire and the Grizzly Bear hits the ground – KERBLAAM!!! Now if you are ignorant enough to immediately run over to the bear – plop down on his chest and holler to your buddy and say: "Hey! Shoot me a Polaroid there Billy Bob."

You might be right in the middle of what you call a "premature celebration" because the Bear might just be knocked down BUT not dead. What you should do {and most hunters with the brains God gave a Billy Goat would do} is shoot him about two or three more times for good measure – cautiously walk over and kick him a couple of times to really make sure he is dead. THEN SHOOT THE POLAROID...

[51] David ran and stood over him. He took hold of the Philistine's sword and drew it from the sheath. After he killed him, he cut off his head with the sword.

Key Number 18

Can you imagine how much dust it would kick up and how loud of a noise it would make when an almost ten foot tall – fully armored giant who had been knocked in the head hit the ground – KERBLAAM!!! Can you imagine the gasps and the screams of unbelief that must have rained down off the hill where the enemy soldiers had been stationed? Even more, can you imagine the tumultuous cheering and saber rattling and accolades that poured down the hill toward David for his "APPARENT" victory from HIS fellow soldiers on the opposite Hill. This could have been the perfect set up for a "premature celebration" by David. I can see it now as he turns all his attention to his "adoring crowd of fans" on the hill – and begins to celebrate with them. Pumping his fists in the air and jumping up and down with excitement he begins to declare: "Yeah, I'm the man. I'm numero uno. I'm the baddest dude on the block. I kicked the enemies butt – big time! Then all of a sudden the once upon a time Hill of Celebration falls silent. Only a few gasps remain. And David confused by the sudden end of the celebration says: Hey! What's wrong guys? Well, I'll tell you what's wrong. While David and his men were deep in their celebration the enemy rose to his feet. He had only been knocked down but not killed. And right now he is about to do a number on David with his big giant sword. <u>BUT</u> the good news is that the wisdom of God prevailed and prior to ANY celebration, David walked over <u>and lopped the Giants head off with a sword.</u> That folks is what you call a "confirmed defeat." THIS giant problem won't be leaving the battle field or coming back to it – EVER!

***It is vitally important that you and I fully understand that as we go through the process of defeating the destructive things that have come against us in life, that we must be <u>absolutely sure</u> that we have dealt with them in such a way that they are GONE, DEAD and BURIED – never to rise again. Don't be satisfied to just knock down the destructive behaviors in your life – MAKE SURE YOU HAVE CUT THE HEAD OFF OF THEM!

When the Philistines saw that their hero was dead, they turned and ran. [52] Then the men of Israel and Judah surged forward with a shout and pursued the Philistines to the entrance of Gath and to the gates of Ekron. Their dead were strewn along the Shaaraim road to Gath and Ekron.

Key Number 19

***My personal life experience coupled with almost twenty years of watching the experiences of the people I have been blessed enough to minister too at our Addiction Recovery Centers for Men and Women is that broken, hurting, frightened and discouraged people are led to victory in their lives more quickly and effectively by others who were also once broken, hurting, frightened and discouraged people themselves <u>BUT</u> have gotten free and <u>STAYED FREE</u>.

*"And the bones came to life and stood up on their feet—<u>**a vast army**</u>."*

My observation is that there is an Army rising up. Not an army of Theologians or Religious Fanatics or Psychiatrists or Psychologists but an Army of Men and Women who are sick and tired of living their life "sick and tired." They are an army that has been lied to most of their lives and know they have spent entirely too much time lying to themselves about what they have become and what they have caused. Because of that - they are hungry for the truth. And they are discovering in droves that the truth they have been searching and longing for is THE TRUTH OF GOD. Look at what happened when just one little shepherd boy named David wandered into a valley full of broken, hurting, frightened and discouraged soldiers. On the heels of his brave stand to face and defeat the ominous enemy that none of them would rise to fight – those who followed the defeated evil giant scattered like a band of cock roaches. And conversely those men in David's camp following his example, his faith and his commitment all followed him off the hill that held them hostage and chased their enemy down a ten mile stretch of road until they killed them all.

What the Army of God needs now more than ever is a bunch more David's – David's that are willing to escape their past, armor up and stand with Christ Jesus to take the Kingdom back from a dead and dying world. If you are broken and hurting today – YOU ARE HIGHLY QUALIFIED to be in the Army of God.

Key Number 20

***When you are fully prepared and ready to walk down into the valley to war against the things that are coming against you in life don't fumble around trying to decide what problem to attack first. Trust me! You need to go after the biggest problem facing you first. WHY? Because just like in David's case - once you defeat the biggest one the little ones will scatter like cock roaches.

In Closing...

Consider beginning immediately to apply the sound principles of living outlined in this book. Then come take your rightful place alongside us on the Battlefield. I often tell the families we minister to: "That the address of Jacob's Well Ministries used to be 45 Buford Lane Poplarville, Mississippi but now the address of Jacob's Well is wherever the hearts and minds are of the thousands of men and women who have gotten free here and stayed free there. Just as God blessed me to once to sit in a room, one on one, and give a hurting person the same living hope God gave me – those same persons are now sitting in a room one on one passing that same living hope on to someone else.

PART SIX
HILL MAN VS VALLEY MAN TEST

Just for fun – Based on the lesson of David and Goliath

Are you a "Hill Man or a "Valley Man

{TAKE THE TEST}

"Hill Man"

*Like to choose "<u>where</u>" they fight their battles.

* Believe there is "<u>safety in numbers</u>."

*Are willing to "<u>take sides</u>" in an argument as long as they don't have to "<u>take a stand</u>."

*Don't mind a "<u>confrontation</u>" as long as they are on "<u>one hill and the enemy is on the other with a valley in between</u>."

*They are most comfortable when they have "<u>someone else</u>" doing their fighting for them.

*Are willing to place their lives, their future and their freedom in the "<u>hands of fate</u>."

*They are easily intimidated, dismayed and terrified by "<u>appearance</u>" and seldom consider "<u>substance</u>."

*They would rather "<u>wallow in their present circumstances</u>" {no matter how unpleasant or terrifying} than "<u>come forward</u>" to meet them enemy face to face.

*Believe that "<u>observing the battle</u>" qualifies them as "<u>part of the battle.</u>"

*Often "<u>burn with jealously and anger</u>" at those who have the courage to fight the battle when they do not.

*Are compelled to act only when "<u>victory</u>" is certain.

*Unfortunately, there are many more "<u>Hill People</u>" in this world than "<u>Valley People.</u>"

"Valley Man"

*Come from the most "<u>unlikely places, circumstances and backgrounds.</u>"

*Are "<u>ready, willing and able</u>" to respond to an immediate need or call.

*"<u>See, hear, feel and respond to challenges</u>" that confront them in life diametrically different than "Hill People" do.

*Are much more interested in the "<u>principle or reason</u>" for the battle than the "<u>material rewards</u>" that might be received for winning it.

*Will not allow themselves to be "<u>discouraged, dismayed or intimidated</u>" by the negative, mean-spirited, hateful comments of those who don't have the courage to fight for what they believe in.

*Have a willingness to "<u>step up to the plate</u>" in any situation {not matter how critical} where it is felt the "<u>cause in worth fighting for</u>."

* Has an "<u>unshakeable confidence</u>" in knowing that the same God who has delivered them from every shameful, disgraceful, dangerous and seemingly impossible situation in life will also deliver them from the challenge they now face.

*Never lets someone else tell them "<u>how they should fight their battles</u>" but rather fights their battles with "<u>the armor God has given them</u>."

*Knows that "<u>the final confrontation</u>" of the battle will seem the most intimidating.

*Understands that the enemy, no matter how intimidating, has "<u>no authority</u>" over those who "<u>stand up for righteousness</u>."

*Never shrink from death but rather "<u>run quickly toward the battle line</u>" when the cause of freedom, righteousness and the glory of the Kingdom are at stake; knowing, that in reality, this is "<u>the Lords battle</u>" not theirs.

*Never claim victory just because the enemy has been "<u>knocked to the ground</u>" but rather **claim victory** only when they have "<u>stood over the enemy, drawn the sword and cut off his head.</u>"

PART SEVEN
EPILOGUE
What I Used to Believe

***I believed a relationship with God {if there was one} would "rain on my parade" concerning the way I wanted to live my life.

*** I believed I was smart enough to get through this life successfully living by my own craftiness without help from anybody on Earth or in Heaven.

*** I believed if I ever did need advice on a problem I could find someone else as devious as I was to partner up with me to help me get what I wanted.

***I believed I was the "center of the universe."

***I believed that the terrible consequences that I often found myself in due to the bad life choices I was making were just the product of "bad luck."

***I believed that there is no problem {no matter how big} I can't run from.

***I believed that the more people I could find to join with me in the bad behaviors I practiced the more "OK" it made the bad behavior.

BUT {WHEN I FACED <u>MY</u> "ROCK BOTTOM MOMENT"} I BEGAN TO REALIZE THAT WHAT I HAD BELIEVED ALL THOSE YEARS WAS A PACK OF LIES AND DISCOVERED THE UNDENIABLE TRUTH THAT:

"The measure of your success in life is not determined by what you *have* done. On the contrary, it is determined by what you have done *about* what you have done"…

IT WAS BECAUSE OF THAT REVELATION THAT I BEGAN TO BELIEVE WHAT I BELIEVE AND LIVE BY TODAY..

Here Is The <u>Real Truth</u> I Came To Believe…

What I Believe Today...

***I believe that there is only one God and His name is **Yahweh**.

***I believe that He is the Creator of all things in Heaven and Earth.

***I believe that He is the God of Abraham, Isaac and Jacob.

***I believe that He is the Lord and Father my Savior Christ Jesus.

***I believe that He loved me so much that He sent "His only begotten Son" to this world to suffer and die on the Cross of Calvary so that {even though I had lived a sinful life} I would not perish but have ever lasting life.

***I believe that my Savior's name is **Yeshua**.

***I believe that He suffered on the Cross at Calvary for my sin and my sake.

***I believe He died there, was buried and was subsequently raised from the dead.

***I believe that He ultimately ascended into Heaven where He sits even now at the right hand of the Father interceding for me against the Accuser of this world.

***I believe that in His absence he has placed a deposit in me called the Holy Spirit of God who will guide me, teach me, correct me, rebuke me and guide me through life on this earth until I will go to spend eternity with Him in Heaven.

***I believe as a Christian that I should believe and receive His Word as given us in the Old and New Testament writings from Genesis 1:1 to the end of Revelation and **apply them** to my life daily.

***I believe that the only way to be given the assurance of eternal salvation is to declare my sins, repent of them, confess with my mouth that Christ is Lord of my life {by that I mean has COMPLETE authority over my life} and believe in my heart that He was truly raised from the dead.

***I believe that my Father in Heaven expects me to offer myself up to Him for the rest of my life as a living sacrifice, Holy and pleasing to him; to turn my back on the ways of the world and conform to them no longer; to allow my mind to be transformed and renewed by a constant washing in the Word so that I might discover His plan and purpose for my life and become a walking living testimony to His Mercy Grace and Power.

I believe that I should determine to **BELIEVE GOD'S WORD** not just believe **IN** GOD'S WORD

THEREFORE I BELIEVE: I AM who this Word says I am. I HAVE what this word says I have.

And, I can DO what this Word says I can do.

That is – "To make the FINAL CHOICE on how to live the rest of my life"

www.ingramcontent.com/pod-product-compliance
Lightning Source LLC
Chambersburg PA
CBHW060950040426
42445CB00011B/1083